Jam Session

Jeff Gordon

Terri Dougherty
ABDO Publishing Company

visit us at
www.abdopub.com

Published by ABDO Publishing Company, 4940 Viking Drive, Suite 622, Edina, Minnesota 55435.
Copyright © 1999 by Abdo Consulting Group, Inc. International copyrights reserved in all countries. No part of this book may be reproduced in any form without written permission from the publisher.

Printed in the United States.

Cover and Interior Photo credits: AP/Wide World Photos

Edited by Denis Dougherty

Sources: Associated Press; Boys' Life; Forbes; Knight-Ridder; Milwaukee Journal Sentinel; Newsweek; People; Sport; Sports Illustrated

Library of Congress Cataloging-in-Publication Data

Dougherty, Terri.
    Jeff Gordon / Terri Dougherty.
       p. cm. -- (Jam Session)
    Includes index.
    Summary: A biography of the race car driver who, at the age of twenty-seven, has captured three NASCAR Winston Cup titles.
     ISBN 1-57765-355-6 (hardcover)
     ISBN 1-57765-357-2 (paperback)
    1. Gordon, Jeff, 1971- Juvenile literature.   2. Automobile racing drivers--United States Biography Juvenile literature. [1. Gordon, Jeff, 1971-- . 2. Automobile racing drivers.]
    I. Title II. Series.
    GV1032.G67D68 1999
    796.72'092--dc21
    [B]   99-25021
                                            CIP

Contents

Unintimidated

The two racers rocketed around the track at 190 miles per hour, Jeff Gordon's rainbow-colored No. 24 car just ahead of Dale Earnhardt's menacing black No. 3.

Stock car racing's young superstar was going bumper to bumper with the legendary Earnhardt in a riveting duel of Chevrolet Monte Carlos. The drivers were battling during the final laps of the Daytona 500, the crown jewel of stock car racing.

Earnhardt is known as The Intimidator because of his tough attitude on the racetrack. He wasn't giving Jeff any room to make a mistake.

The crafty Earnhardt took his foot off the gas pedal a tiny bit to give himself room to pass Jeff. Jeff knew what the veteran driver was trying to do and slowed just enough so Earnhardt couldn't get around him.

Jeff Gordon crosses the finish line ahead of Dale Earnhardt to win the 1999 Daytona 500.

As they neared the finish, Jeff weaved toward the wall and then the grass to prevent Earnhardt from passing him. He zoomed across the finish line to win the Daytona 500 for the second time in three years.

"Those were the longest laps I've ever run around Daytona," Jeff said after he beat Earnhardt on the thrilling afternoon of February 14, 1999. "He was setting me up every single lap, trying to get by me, and I really thought he was going to get me. What an awesome, awesome race."

The exciting victory at the fabled Daytona International Speedway at Daytona Beach, Florida, was all in a day's work for Jeff, who has rocketed to the top of the racing world.

Jeff celebrates in Victory Lane after winning the 1999 Daytona 500.

By age 27, Jeff had captured three NASCAR Winston Cup Series points championships. He is the youngest driver to win more than 40 races and three season championships. In 1998, he became the first driver in the modern era to have 10 or more victories three years in a row.

"The kid's a flat-out, natural-born racer," Earnhardt said early in Jeff's NASCAR career. "If he sticks with it, he'll break every record I've ever set."

Team members congratulate Jeff after winning the 1999 Daytona 500.

The Boy Is Up to Speed

Jeff's mother and father divorced when Jeff was very young. Jeff's mother, Carol, then married John Bickford. Jeff lived with his mother and stepfather in Vallejo, California.

Jeff always craved speed. When he was three years old, he would take his bike to the top of a hill near his family's home and zoom to the bottom. Then he'd do it again and again. When he was four, he started racing bikes against other kids. But his mother thought bike racing was too dangerous so he turned to car racing.

Jeff's stepfather owned an auto parts company that made car parts for disabled people. He made many of the parts for Jeff's cars. At age five, Jeff put on an official racing uniform and drove a small race car. "Once I realized, 'Hey, I can control this car,' I was fascinated by it," Jeff said.

Jeff's first race car was a quarter midget his stepfather built for $450. The engine was about as powerful as a lawn mower engine. The six-foot-long car was built like a go-kart, but had a cover over the driver. The family began traveling all over the country so Jeff could race. Before long, all Jeff did was race.

"Most kids in quarter midgets race maybe 20 weekends a year," Jeff's stepfather said. "We raced 52 weekends a year, somewhere in the United States. We had eight or nine cars. We practiced two or three times a week. The laps he drove when he was six or seven years old, he's still applying them."

Jeff won 36 quarter-midget races his second year. When he was eight, he was the Grand National Champion among quarter-midget racers.

Young Jeff Gordon gets ready to race as his stepfather looks on.

When he was nine, Jeff decided to try something different. He began racing go-karts, which have more powerful engines. The results were the same: he kept winning. "All the other parents were saying Jeff was probably lying about his age, that he was probably 20 and just real little," his stepfather said. "Nobody wanted to race us. That was fine. We moved up to the junior class. These kids were 13 to 17, and he was killing them."

Jeff was successful but wanted to test his skills against tougher competition. He moved up to superstock light, which has higher horsepower. "Now we were running against guys 17 and older, unlimited age," his stepfather said. "We were still winning."

But the older drivers didn't like getting beat by a young boy. Jeff won all 25 go-kart events he entered at age 10, but returned to quarter-midget racing where he felt more welcomed. He won a second national quarter-midget title when he was 10 and began to wonder where he would find his next challenge.

Jeff was a champion racer before he was a teenager, beating people nearly twice his age.

"You get to be 12 years old," Jeff recalled, "and you realize you've been in quarter midgets for eight years. What's next? I was getting older, not knowing what I wanted to do next."

Putting His Foot Down in Stock Cars

Jeff found what he was looking for in sprint cars. Sprint cars are bigger than quarter midgets but smaller than ordinary race cars. At some racetracks there were no rules about how old a driver has to be.

"Nobody was fool enough to drive that young, so they didn't think they needed an age rule," Jeff's stepfather said.

Jeff and his stepfather built their first sprint car for $25,000. When Jeff was 13, he trained with the All-Star circuit on its winter tour in Florida. In 1986, Jeff's family moved to Indiana so the 14-year-old could race there.

"We slept in pickup trucks and made our own parts," Jeff's stepfather recalled.

Jeff drove 650-horsepower sprint cars on half-mile dirt tracks. He won three sprint races before he was old enough to get an Indiana driver's license. By the time he turned 16, he was beating drivers more than twice his age.

He started racing regularly on the U.S. Automobile Club sprint-car circuit at 18, driving 815-horsepower, open-wheel sprinters. He also won the USAC season championship in full midgets.

Jeff has credited legendary racer Buddy Baker (left) and his dad Buck for making him a better racer.

He attracted interest from Jackie Stewart, a top driver who won the Formula One championship three times. Stewart wanted Jeff to drive on his son's team in Europe. But Jeff couldn't get a sponsor, so he stayed in the United States.

In the summer of 1990, Jeff's mother and stepfather encouraged him to look into stock cars. He attended a driving school conducted by former NASCAR star Buck Baker in Rockingham, North Carolina.

"That first day, the first time I got in a [stock] car, I said, 'This is it. This is what I want to do,'" Jeff recalled. "The car was different from anything that I was used to. It was so big and heavy. It felt very fast but very smooth. I loved it."

The stock cars Jeff drives have the shape of an ordinary car, but underneath they are very different. A stock car has more safety equipment, like a roll bar to protect the driver in a crash. It also has a very powerful engine. A normal car has 200 horsepower. Stock cars have up to 700 horsepower.

"In a street car you have to get on the gas pretty hard just to get up to 55 or 65 m.p.h.," Jeff said. "In my car I can do 65 in first gear and 100 easily in second, and I've still got two more gears to go!"

Races and Romance

Jeff's mastery of the racetrack continued with stock cars. In 1991, he entered the Busch Series, the second-highest level in NASCAR. He captured the USAC Silver Crown championship for open-wheel cars and was the Busch Series Rookie of the Year.

At a Busch race in Atlanta the next season, Jeff's aggressive driving style caught the eye of Rick Hendrick. Hendrick was the owner of the biggest, richest team in the Winston Cup Series, the top level of NASCAR.

"I caught this white car out of the corner of my eye," Hendrick recalled. "I said, 'Man, that guy's gonna wreck!' Dale Earnhardt and Harry Gant were leading, and this white car was right up on them. But the [white] car went on to win the race. I asked who the driver was. Somebody said, 'That's that kid Gordon.'"

When Hendrick met Jeff, he couldn't believe how nice the successful young driver was. "I was almost in a daze," Hendrick said. "Jeff had it all. It was just scary. He's good-looking, and I couldn't believe how well he handled himself at age 20. What I found was a mature young guy who was kind of humble, a little bashful."

Jeff signed with Hendrick later that season and entered his first Winston Cup race in November 1992. At the beginning of the next season, Jeff became the first rookie in 30 years and the youngest driver to win a 125-mile qualifying race for the Daytona 500.

But after the victory, his mind wasn't on the race. He was awestruck by the beautiful model who gave him the trophy, Brooke Sealey. "I was wowed before I ever met her," Jeff said.

Team owner Rick Hendrick (left) and crew chief Ray Evernham congratulate Jeff after his great qualifying run for the 1999 Daytona 500.

Race car drivers aren't supposed to date the models who hand out the trophies, but Jeff and Brooke dated in secret for a year. At the end of the season, Jeff was named the 1993 Winston Cup Rookie of the Year. He also revealed his romance. He and Brooke married the next year and moved into a house on Lake Norman, outside Charlotte, North Carolina.

"Women come up to me all the time and say, 'You're so lucky you got him before I could,'" Brooke said. "I just laugh. I agree with them."

Jeff with wife Brooke after winning the ACDelco 400 in 1998.

On the Fast Track to Success

The racing world was poised for a big change in the summer of 1994. Stock cars were going to race at the historic Indianapolis Motor Speedway for the first time in its 85-year existence. On August 6, just two days after turning 23, Jeff revved his engine in the first Brickyard 400.

With four laps left in the 160-lap race, Jeff and Ernie Irvan were in the lead. They rounded the turn side-by-side. Suddenly, Irvan's tire exploded, his car slowed, and Jeff was all alone in front.

"Oh man, what a battle," Jeff said. "We had a great battle all day long."

Jeff's pit crew, known as the Rainbow Warriors, push out the car before a race.

Crewmen from other teams gave him high fives and showed him victory signs as Jeff drove down pit road.

"We've got a great driver," said Jeff's crew chief, Ray Evernham. "The kid is just phenomenal."

The next season, Jeff didn't relax and revel in his success. He kept focusing on his next race. "I don't sit and think, 'Man, can I win seven championships, or 10 championships?' I'm just going for that first one," he said.

Jeff had 11 race cars to choose from and the strongest engines on the tour. Evernham and the Rainbow Warriors pit crew were almost perfect on race days. Jeff showed skill in his early season successes, but remained humble.

Another victory for Jeff.

"I'm just a kid," Jeff said. "It's just a big blur, how fast I've gotten to this level. I can't even remember some things."

Jeff's team finished among the top eight cars 20 times in 22 starts between April and October 1995. In the Winston Cup points race, he led Earnhardt by 302 points with four races left. But by the final race of the season, Earnhardt had a good chance of passing him.

"We didn't talk about points or the championship until very late in the season," Jeff said. "We focused on running hard and winning."

Jeff credits his pit crew for much of his success.

Jeff didn't end the season with a bang. He finished 34th in the final race at Atlanta. But it was good enough to give him his first Winston Cup championship.

"This isn't the way we wanted to finish up," Jeff said. "But we wanted to end up the champions, and we did that. If I never win another one, I'll always have this one."

Jeff talks with crew chief Ray Evernham during practice at the 1999 Dura-Lube 400.

Lapping the Competition

Although Jeff was a humble winner, some veteran NASCAR drivers weren't friendly. Fans sometimes booed NASCAR's "wonder boy" because they felt he hadn't earned his success.

"I don't take it personally," Jeff said. "I take it almost as a compliment. I'm doing something they don't want me to do, something that's not making them happy."

"I've had to learn a lot of things very quickly," Jeff said, "and I try to learn from [my] mistakes. You've got to fight hard to win a championship, and [in 1995] we all did it as a team together."

Jeff remained focused on winning. In 1995 and 1996, Jeff won 17 out of 62 races, more than the next two top drivers combined. In 1996, he had a 111-point lead in the points race with four races to go, but lost the crown to Terry Labonte by 37 points.

"We were all happy for him," Jeff said the next season. "Losing last year only made our team stronger."

Jeff opened the 1997 season with a big victory at the Daytona 500 in February. He was the star of every big race that season and became the first driver to have back-to-back seasons with at least 10 victories since Darrell Waltrip in 1981 and 1982.

"I can get the job done as well as anybody out there," Jeff said.

The points chase again came down to the wire. Jeff was nervous before the final race, the NAPA 500 in Atlanta.

"I said I'd been sleeping well, but I haven't slept in two weeks," Jeff admitted. Jeff made several mistakes during practice, and it looked like he might lose the title. As he was swerving his Monte Carlo left and right to warm up the tires, he lost control, spun 180 degrees, and hit Bobby Hamilton's parked Grand Prix.

Jeff's car was so badly damaged his team had to use a backup. Then, during a qualifying race that would determine where Jeff's car would start the NAPA 500, his rear tires slipped in oil. Jeff had to slow down and started the race 37th.

Crew members and the media surround Jeff Gordon's car in Victory Lane after winning the 1999 Daytona 500.

Jeff had to finish 18th or better to win the championship. Toward the end of the race he was 17th, and he just hoped his tires would hold out and allow him to finish.

"Even when they waved the white flag [signaling one lap left in the race], I wasn't comfortable because I was afraid a tire could blow at any moment," Jeff said. "Only when I came off turn four on the last lap, and knew that I could get to the line even if a tire went, did I sigh in relief."

Jeff claimed the title by 14 points over Dale Jarrett. "Our team motto is 'Refuse to Lose'," Jeff said. "We won 10 races for the past two seasons, and that just seems incredible."

Bobby Labonte, who won the NAPA 500 that year, predicted more titles for Jeff. "He's done it before," Labonte said. "And I'm sure he'll do it again. His team is awesome."

"Out of the car, he's like a junior high school kid," driver Kyle Petty said. "But inside the car, he's a fierce competitor. Whatever it takes to win, that's what he does."

Jeff waves to fans before the start of the NAPA 500.

Cheers at the Brickyard

In 1998, Jeff heard the only thing that had been lacking in his racing career: wild cheers from fans. Jeff considers Pittsboro, Indiana, his hometown. And the hometown fans were on his side when he returned to Indianapolis for the 1998 Brickyard 400. Jeff pleased them by winning the biggest purse in auto-racing history, more than $1.6 million.

"After the race, as I drove down pit road, I shut the engine off, because I just had to hear it," Jeff said. "I don't hear a roar like that anywhere else."

Jeff dominated that season. He tied Richard Petty's modern-era record with 13 victories. He won so often people began to wonder if he was cheating by using a special chemical on his tires. But NASCAR investigated and cleared Jeff of any wrongdoing.

Jeff Gordon holds the Winston Cup after winning the 1998 NAPA 500 and becoming the Winston Cup champion.

Other owners had another explanation for Jeff's success. "I think Jeff Gordon is the best stock car driver of all time," said rival team owner Felix Sabates. "I think he's got the best crew of all time."

"Everybody says they're cheating, but they're not," said Richard Childress, who has Earnhardt driving for his team. "They've got a good thing going, good cars, good people, a good engine program and a good race driver and good crew chief, the whole package."

Jeff didn't fade toward the end of the season. He won three of his last four races, including the season-finale at Atlanta. With his third title, he was on his way to topping Richard Petty and Earnhardt's shared record of seven championships.

"If I have years like I've had this year, I'll race as long as I possibly can," Jeff said. "I don't put an age or a number on it. It has to do with being competitive and being in shape."

Crew members move fast during a pit stop.

No Slowing Down

As the 1999 season began, Jeff was poised to become the first winner of three straight Winston Cup crowns since Cale Yarborough in 1976-78.

"What motivates Jeff is the next race," Evernham said. "It seems like the better you do, the more you get motivated."

Jeff hasn't let success tarnish his clean image. "I don't do drugs. I don't smoke and I have a wonderful wife who keeps me very grounded," Jeff said. "It's pretty easy to stay out of trouble. I'm not a very good liar, so if I was doing that I wouldn't be able to live with the guilt."

Confetti flies after Jeff wins the 1999 Daytona 500.

Jeff's incredible ability may be matched only by his humility. He routinely credits God for his accomplishments and insists he's just one part of a highly talented and motivated team.

"As long as we can stay focused and stay together and continue to grow, I feel like we can stay competitive," Jeff said. "But I also feel like some of these other teams are going to make things really tough on us. Them pushing us makes us strive to make ourselves better.

"I feel like this sport is just taking off," Jeff added. "And I'm really proud to be a part of that."

Jeff gives the thumbs up after taking the pole position for the Daytona 500 in 1999.

Jeff Gordon Profile

Born: August 4, 1971

Hometown: Pittsboro, Indiana

Height: 5-foot-7

Weight: 150 pounds

Family: Wife, Brooke

Crew Chief: Ray Evernham

Car Owner: Rick Hendrick

Personal:

• Jeff's first competitor was his mother, Carol, who raced against him during practices on a makeshift racetrack in Vallejo, California.

• His stepfather, John Bickford, marketed the first Jeff Gordon T-shirts when Jeff was eight.

• Jeff became bored by racing at age 12 and became so interested in waterskiing that he considered turning pro.

Jeff Gordon's Honors

Grand National champion in quarter midgets: 1979 and 1981

USAC full-midget Rookie of the Year: 1989

USAC season champion in full midgets: 1990

Busch Series Rookie of the Year: 1991

Winston Cup Rookie of the Year: 1993

Winston Cup champion: 1995, 1997, 1998

Jeff Gordon Chronology

1971 - Born on August 4 in Vallejo, California

1977 - Gets his first race car, a quarter midget. Wins Western States Championship in his class, and fast time award.

1979 - Wins his first Grand National Championship in quarter midgets. Wins Pacific Northwest Indoor championships.

1981 - Wins second Grand National Championship quarter-midget title.

1984 - Trains with sprint car All-Star circuit in Florida.

1986 - Moves to Indiana.

1989 - Wins USAC Midget Rookie of the Year award.

1990 - Wins USAC season championship in full midgets. Drives a stock car for the first time.

Jeff Gordon takes time to sign a few autographs.

1991 - Enters NASCAR Busch Series. Named Busch Series Rookie of the Year.

1992 - First NASCAR Winston Cup race. Wins $6,285.

1993 - 30 races, 7 top five finishes, 11 top 10 finishes. Ends season fourth in points standings, one pole position. Wins $765,168.

1994 - 31 races, 2 wins, 7 top five finishes, 14 top 10 finishes, 1 pole position. Ends season eighth in points standings. Wins first Brickyard 400. Wins $1,779,523.

1995 - 31 races, 7 wins, 17 top five finishes, 23 top 10 finishes, 8 pole positions. Ends season first in points standings. Wins $4,347,343.

1996 - 31 races, 10 wins, 21 top five finishes, 24 top 10 finishes, 5 pole positions. Ends season second in points standings. Wins $3,428,485.

1997 - 32 races, 10 wins, 22 top five finishes, 23 top 10 finishes, 1 pole position. Ends season first in points standings. Wins $6,375,658.

1998 - 33 races, 13 wins, 26 top five finishes, 28 top 10 finishes, 7 pole positions. Ends season first in points standings. Wins a record $9.3 million.

1999 - Wins the Daytona 500 on February 14.

Glossary

DAYTONA 500 - A 200-lap, 500-mile race at Daytona International Speedway in Daytona Beach, Florida. The most prestigious event on the NASCAR Winston Cup Series schedule.

FULL MIDGET - Race car weighing about 925 pounds with a 320-horsepower engine.

GO-KART - Small car with no cover over the driver; usually has a small engine and is limited to slow speeds.

M.P.H. - Miles per hour; measures how fast a car goes.

NASCAR - National Association for Stock Car Auto Racing; founded by Bill France in 1948; organizes and promotes stock car races.

PIT CREW - Mechanics who work quickly on a car during a race. They change tires, refuel, and make repairs.

POLE POSITION - The car lined up at the inside, front-row position on the starting line for a race.

QUARTER MIDGET - Six-foot race car with a single-cylinder, 2.85 horsepower engine.

SPRINT CAR - A race car smaller than a stock car but with the same power; usually races on a dirt track.

STOCK CAR - Race car with the basic body of a street car but with many more safety features and a 700 horsepower engine; it has one seat, no speedometer, webbing in place of a driver's side window, and a door welded shut; the driver enters through the window.

WINSTON CUP SERIES - Top series of races for stock car drivers.

Index